WRITING ON THE INTERNET

LEARN SEO TIPS & TECHNIQUES AND BECOME A SUCCESSFUL ONLINE WRITER

BY SMART READS

Free Audiobook

As a thank you for being a Smart Reader you can choose 2 FREE audiobooks from audible.com. Simply sign up for free by visiting www.audibletrial.com/Travis to get your books.

Visit:
www.smartreads.co/freebooks
to receive Smart Reads books for FREE

Check us out on Instagram:
www.instagram.com/smart_readers
@smart_readers

ABOUT SMARTREADS

Choose Smart Reads and get smart every time. Smart Reads sorts through all the best content and condenses the most helpful information into easily digestible chunks.

We design our books to be short, easy to read and highly informative. Leaving you with maximum understanding in the least amount of time.

Smart Reads aims to accelerate the spread of quality information so we've taken the copyright off everything we publish and donate our material directly to the public domain. You can read our uncopyright below.

We believe in paying it forward and donate 5% of our net sales to Pencils of Promise to build schools, train teachers and support child education.

To limit our footprint and restore forests around the globe we are planting a tree for every 10 hardcover books we sell.

Thanks for choosing Smart Reads and helping us help the planet.

Sincerely,

Travis & the Smart Reads Team

TABLE OF CONTENTS

INTRODUCTION

"Making money is art, and working is art, and good business is the best art."
- Andy Warhol

Copy writing has never been more in demand. And because it's so much in demand, people are willing to pay a LOT of money for the best talent. Pretty soon, you will be part of the cream of the crop who can ask for princely sums in exchange for red-hot copy. Countless people have done it and so can you.

You only need three things to get started:

• A laptop (or a computer)
• Wi-Fi
• And good writing skills

At first, you might think that becoming a freelance writer sounds tricky and even daunting. Maybe you still feel that way about it. People can feel especially nervous about becoming a freelance writer if they have no journalistic or literary background or qualifications. But guess what? None of that matters.

Copy writing is different from both journalistic and literary writing. And indeed, some of the best novelist and poets would struggle to succeed as a copywriter.

There is nothing - with possibly the exception of a basic understanding of grammar - that a degree in the English language can help you with when it comes to copywriting. Instead, the rules you've learned are about to be broken.

CHAPTER 1: WHAT TYPE OF WRITING ARE WE TALKING ABOUT HERE?

SEO writing. Ever heard of that? SEO stands for Search Engine Optimization. What does this mean?

When someone says an article is SEO optimized, it means that it contains keywords (or topics) that people are actively searching for in Google. Let's say you write an article about leather jackets and a client tells you that the keyword is "discounted men's leather jackets." You're asked to use this keyword six times throughout the article as this will ensure that Google ranks it fairly highly.

When people come along and tap, "discounted men's leather jackets" into Google, lo and behold your article is the first thing they see. Writers that don't care for keywords will find it tough to get their content seen. Google ranks content according to how good their SEO is. Get yours spot on - which is super easy to do - and you climb up the Google search rankings.

Not all your clients will request that you use keywords. In fact, a lot won't. But when they do, they'll want you to use the keywords organically so that it doesn't look like a machine wrote it.

Here's how NOT to do SEO:

"Come visit our store for some discounted men's leather jackets. We've got the best discounted men's leather jackets for anyone who loves a bargain. As well as discounted men's leather jackets, we also have ..."

It looks horrible. Not pretty and completely unreadable. You have to be sparing with your use of keywords and fit them into your content so that it always looks natural.

When writing SEO content, you need to do two things:

• Inform your audience with entertaining, engaging content
• Maximize the articles' search engine ranking

At first, you might find it hard to balance the two. But with practice, it'll become second nature.

SEO is easy to get into for beginners, and you might find it's the niche you enter first. This is because it doesn't pay a ton, and the clients who need it are usually small business owners who work in unusual niches. For example, you might find yourself writing articles for a dentist in Minnesota one minute and articles for a pet store in Scotland the next.

It's not always the most interesting line of work, and you always have to be mindful of where you're placing the keywords and avoid keyword stuffing (using too many keywords, which Google condemns as spam).

The good news is that SEO articles are generally no longer than 500 words. Sometimes they're 1,000, but that still isn't a lot. You've just got to make sure to write content that is informative but also engaging. Basically, not too dry but also not too "bloggy." You need to make sure you use the keyword that your client gives you in the right amount of times and in the right place.

It's good practice to use the keyword once in the first line, once in a sub-header, a few times throughout the article (usually two times), and then again in the last line.

CHAPTER 2: HOW TO TRIPLE HOURLY EARNINGS VIA SEO WRITING

Don't be surprised if the only jobs offered to you as a newbie is SEO writing, will be a job that pays poorly. There are some clients who take advantage of this and say, "You don't have much experience but we LOVE to give newbie writers a chance." So they give you a platform in exchange for you accepting pretty lousy fees.

In many ways, this works out fine and dandy for you. You ARE getting a platform in which you can test the waters and hone your skills. And you're doing it without the pressure of a massive fee dangling around your neck. Sure, $5 for 500 words might seem like a pittance. But there's barely any pressure at all, and the chances are high that the client isn't expecting a totally flawless effort. They just want some content. Plus, guess what? The client is right - you DON'T have any experience.

Experience must be earned. And if that means working a few lousy-paying jobs for a few weeks while you build your stamina, resolve and skills, then so be it. Yeah? Moreover, remember that if you can dust off 4 x 500 word articles an hour that pay $5 each, that's $20.

Which is still more than the average national minimum wage. So you're still winning.

But what if you don't want to write so much at first? Are there better ways of making money from writing without actually having to write yourself? There is. Some people would outsource their work. A common practice is for them to apply for writing jobs on writing or job platforms like Freelancer.com or Upwork.com. Then they would also hire other writers and outsource the writing work then split the pay. While you could do this as well, remember that you will still need to work on and proofread the writers' work yourself. What's more, in some instances, you'll need to do a fair amount of editing.

However, if you're a slow typist who can't knock out 4 x 500 words an hour, it probably sounds like an attractive proposition. Especially if you're good at getting jobs and know good writers.

Let's say you find jobs that pay $20 per 1,000 words and you land the job. You hand the article over to another writer. They take $10 and you take $10. That sounds like a pretty fair deal, right? After all, it was your expertise that got the job and it's you that will be editing the work. Plus, it's your reputation at stake.

Moreover, finding clients is hard. It certainly isn't easy. Indeed, most writers will admit that the thing they struggle the most with is finding leads. It's arguably one of the hardest - if not the hardest - aspect of being a freelancer.

If you do go this route, the more you do this - and the more writers you can leverage - the more money you can make on the side.

Bear in mind, you WILL need to check the articles. If you don't, you could be handing in poor-quality work that hurts your ratings. And if you lose ratings on a global freelancing platform such as Upwork.com, you will struggle to secure future work. At that point, you won't even be able to get jobs for yourself, let alone your writers.

CHAPTER 3: HOW TO FIND PREMIUM SEO WRITING CLIENTS

As mentioned, finding clients is one of the hardest parts of being a freelance writer. It's all well and good to say you want to become a freelancer. But where are your employers going to come from? You won't find them in the office anymore!

While it can be challenging to find clients when starting out, it does get easier once you've built up a roster of clients and gain experience. Lowballer clients will always be around and while you can use them when starting out, you certainly don't want to be doing 1,000 word articles for $5 forever. That's just not how it goes.

So how do you find premium SEO writing clients? Turns out they're also in the same platform as the lowballer clients, all you have to do is find them. The more you gain in experience, the more confidence you have over your capacity and skills. What's more, it also means you get better at what you're doing and can charge more or your worth. You won't end up charging hundreds of dollars per hour right away but as you get better, you can raise your rate and earn more.

At the same time, you can continue looking for clients that pay much better. They are out there. The articles they require might be different and more tedious but you also grow in skill and experience as you go as you move up. However, the bottom line is that the client is looking for good quality content.

SEO is just a good way of learning the ropes. It gives you a free pass into the world of making easy money online and practically anyone who can spell and string sentences together that are readable and fairly engaging can do it. And really, 500 words is NOT a lot.

Remember when 500-word essays at college sounded like a lot? The big difference is that it was an essay and this is just SEO writing. Trust me, 500 words is a cinch.

Hold Up! What If I Actually Can't Write For Real?
Sure, it's a legitimate concern if you're not sure how to write in the first place. But remember, SEO writing is totally different to any writing you've done before. It's not essay writing, it's not dissertation writing, and there isn't a teacher berating you for all your mistakes and pointing out your run-on sentences.

It's totally different. You're writing a bit of content for a website/small business that wants their page to rank higher on Google so they improve conversions and sales.

Yes, you have to be able to write somewhat adequately. But the more you do it, the better you'll get. For now, take a look at some examples and get a feel for what you need to do.

CHAPTER 4: WHY YOU'RE GOING TO LOVE MAKING MONEY THIS WAY

"I have ways of making money that you know nothing of." – John D. Rockefeller

Okay, so it's a tad arrogant. But so what? He can afford to be arrogant. After all, he knows ways of making money that you don't!

SEO writing is a great way of making a stack of cash that a lot of people don't know about. Ask your friends what they think of SEO writing, and the chances are that they've never heard of it.

So you know you're qualified to get into SEO writing, now let's look at WHY you should get into it.

1. You Can Make A Lot Of Money

If you don't want get stuck on a predictable hourly wage of $15 like your friends, you don't have to. Not if you get into SEO writing. The potential for massive earnings from SEO writing are HUGE. If you can find the right clients, the sky is the limit. When you take any old regular 9-5 job, your hourly rate is always fixed. Let's say you earn $15 an hour. That's not going to change at all unless you get a raise which can be tough especially when you're competing with other employees in the paygrade. Chances are, it won't even change if you work faster and harder and get more stuff done. It will always remain the same, even if your productivity goes up or down. Not so with SEO writing. How fast you can write decides your hourly rate.

Instead of being stuck on $15 an hour, you can make $30 an hour if you are fast and productive. Essentially, you get rewarded for speed, hard work and productivity. Sure, you won't be able to smash out 2,000 words at first. You'll be too busy learning the ropes and dipping your toes in the water. But as time goes on and you do more writing, you really will pick up the pace.

There is another way your hourly wage can go up. Unlike folk working regular 9-5 jobs, you can literally "ask for a raise" whenever you want. Let's say you've been working for one particular client for a month. The client pays just $4 per 500 words. That's lousy money and you know it's lousy money. But you took the job on because it was something.

Moreover, the client was right - you don't have much experience and you're a bit rough around the edges. You're certainly not an all-star just yet. As such, your prices reflect this.

After a month though, you realize you're getting pretty good at this. Confident that you're better than $4 per 500 words, you politely thank the client of the experience and tell them you're moving on to other work. Other work means better paying clients who pay you according to your new worth. And you can keep doing this as you grow your talent. You can literally rise from the bottom to the top, from a poorly-paying client to a well-paying client. Eventually, you might find you've bagged yourself a client who pays a whopping $100 per 1,000 words! Yes, they are out there! And once you've gained experience and polished your craft, these clients open up to you. This isn't something you can do in a regular 9-5 job.

2. There Isn't Much Competition

As mentioned earlier, lots of people still haven't heard of SEO writing. As a result, there isn't that much competition but plenty of work available!

The amount of SEO work available really is staggering. But because there still aren't many good SEO writers out there, it means you can easily enter this sector and make some pretty big strides. And because you're reading this book, you're going to be one of the best writers around.

You're going to be so good that people can't ignore you. It wouldn't even matter if there were competition. Even better is that you'll be paid what you're worth.

3. The Demand For Writers is Only Going To Grow
A lot of people think that eventually the work would dry up. After all, how much content do people really need? What if no one wants written content anymore? What if everyone just wants video?

The reality is that demand for content isn't slowing down at all. In fact, it's growing at a rapid pace and it is only going to keep growing. You're not even entering this at the beginning stage. You're entering this at the pre-beginning stage. That's right. You're entering this sector before things have really taken off.

Written content on the Internet is just getting started. People are still experimenting. And because clients rarely get things right the first time around, you can step in and do it for them the second or third time. Plus, so what if someone uploaded some content last year or last week? Google likes fresh content every single week. It even wants fresh content every single day! The moment websites stop uploading fresh content is the moment they start losing out to their competitors. They know this. They know they need writers like you. And you might argue, "But what if a client already has a freelancer? What if all the clients already have freelancers? I'm basically blockaded from entering this sector."

A client might already have someone writing for them. But they've got so much work available and their writer can't keep up. So what do they do? They hire a second, third and even a fourth freelancer.

Moreover, new clients are popping up all the time. Thanks to the way our world works, there will always be bright, innovative people who are launching new businesses and websites, and who need people like you to write for them.

Lastly, no one is ever going to stop wanting content. Why? Because content makes money. Lots of it. It's a lucrative business. Words sell. And they're going to keep selling.

4. You Can Work When You Want, Where You Want

Easily one of the best things about a writing job is that you can set your own hours. You can also decide where you want to work. Don't fancy working at home today because your family is being too noisy, or your study just doesn't inspire you to write? You don't have to! You're free to go to any public space where there is a Wi-Fi connection and work from there.

And what if you're always at your most productive and come up with your best words at midnight onwards? Then work at night! Lie in bed until 10 AM, coast through the day, spend quality time with your family, watch some sports, before buckling down to work late at night. Office workers don't have this type of flexibility, often to the detriment of the company. But you do. So use it.

5. SEO Writing Is So Easy To Learn
SEO writing is easy to learn. As long as you can string sentences together and know how to engage people, you're on your way. Just remember to be engaging, informative and - where possible - entertaining. Don't be wooden, dry and boring.

These rules are easy to remember. If you find that your writing looks too boring, read a fun blog post. It will help you to understand style and tone, and will inspire you to fire up your own content.

6. No Good With Technology? So What!

You really don't need to be a tech wizard to get into SEO writing. All you need is your computer and WiFi. That's literally it. Oh, and a bank account.

As you get good at SEO writing, you might want to think about launching your own website to sell your services, but it isn't necessary.

CHAPTER 5: SEO JARGON

Most people hate jargon. The worst thing about getting involved in a new sector is that you're thrown terms you've never heard of before. Maybe you didn't even know what SEO meant before reading this book. However, getting acquainted with SEO lingo is an important part of the process if you're going to be successful. The last thing you want is to be on a Skype call with a client when they ask if you have experience with anchor links and you have to mute yourself while you Google.

In this chapter, you'll learn some of the key terms you'll come across, and which clients will expect you to understand when working as an SEO writer. Once you understand these terms, you can start using them in your resume.

Keywords
SEO writing is all about keywords. If a piece of text has no keywords, it isn't SEO.

SEO stands for Search Engine Optimized. Basically, to get a website near the top of Google's search results, its content must contain the right amount of keywords that people are looking for. What's the right amount? About 4% of your text should contain the keyword for it to be optimized. Too much and Google will mark it spam. Too little and it won't rank.

You don't need to be concerned with the science behind keywords. It's not your job to research which ones to use. Your job is simply to slot the keywords a client gives you into a text as seamlessly as possible. Ergo - don't make it obvious to the reader that you're using keywords.

This is an easy trap that first-time SEO writers fall into. When you first start SEO writing, a client gives you a brief outline of what they want the article to be about as well as one or two keywords for you to use. Because you're not sure what the deal is, you use the keywords way too many times, and you use them in inappropriate places. It looks obvious what you're trying to do, and it looks messy and impersonal.

As a general rule, you use keywords no more than 6 times in a 500-word article. For best SEO practice, use a keyword once in the first 20 words and again in the last 20 words. Use it also in at least one sub-heading, and then three times in the rest of the text.

Links
A link takes the reader to another website or page when they click on it. Links are good for SEO because

they improve rankings. Google especially loves you when you use outbound links (links to other websites) because it demonstrates that you're a solid member of the Google community who doesn't want to keep traffic all to yourself.

Also, outbound links are necessary if you're citing studies in an article. Don't just say, "X is this." Include the link that proves it (ergo, where you got the info from. It must be an authoritative site).

Anchor Text
Anchor text is the text that accompanies an outbound link. Anchor text is NOT the link - it's the text that goes over the top of a link.

Let's say that you're writing about weight loss. If you're linking to a study about weight loss, you might present it like this:

"According to research, it was discovered that red meat is linked to weight gain."

Your link would accompany the text colored blue. It's just neat practice. It looks presentable, and lets the reader know where they need to click to find out more info.

URL

Unless you're asked to use WordPress, you won't need to know too much about URLs. For now, all you need to know is that a URL is a websites address, which you'll find in your search engine's address bar.

And that is quite literally it. That's all the jargon you need to know. Not bad, right?
Sometimes a client might throw you a curveball and talk about something you've never heard of before. If they do, don't be shy. Just ask for clarification. It will save you a heck of a lot of potential trouble.

CHAPTER 6: SEVEN SECRET HACKS TO HELP YOU SUCCEED

"Life is really simple, but we insist on making it complicated."
- Confucious

Forget everything you were ever taught about writing. Unlearn all that you learned on a creative writing course. Block everything your teacher taught you in an English language degree. None of that stuff will help you - it will only hinder you.

Back then, you were taught to use long, winding, big fat paragraphs. They might work in a novel or a dissertation. But they're not going to cut it with clients or Internet readers. And all that flowery, poetic language you used that charmed the pants off your teacher and made a girl or boy fall in love with you? Get rid of it. You don't need it here.

1. Stop Writing Long Paragraphs
Learn tostart writing shorter paragraphs. That means 4 sentences in a paragraph maximum. Don't be scared. This is normal. Your content will start to flow better and look better. Internet users don't want to be greeted by walls and walls of text. They want short, snappy, broken-up text that looks like it's easy to read.

2. Use Sub-Headings

Sub-headings guide the readers eye from one part of the text to the other. They help to break the text and make it look readable, and they also allow the reader know exactly what's in the article.

Most Internet users skim through an article first before reading the entire thing. They check the sub-headings to make sure the article has got what they want/need. Your sub-headings must be both catchy and informative, and at least one of them should contain your main keyword. Not everyone who reads an article on the Internet reads every word. Most people don't. Instead, they just scan the sub-headings. As a writer, that might hurt your ego. Don't let it do that. You're only here to do your job and make money.

3. Keep Your Sentences Short

Just like you should keep your paragraphs short, you should also keep your sentences short. Internet users aren't here to read a novel. They have an attention span worse than a gold fish. Can you believe that? An attention span worse than a gold fish! You don't have much time to impress them and keep them on the page. And you'll be impressing nobody if you employ long, unreadable sentences.

Keep things short and concise. If something feels too long, it is too long. If a sentence can easily be broken up into two sentences, go right ahead and break it up into two sentences. If you're a bit unsure about all this, and if it offends your literary background, take a look at some SEO examples on the Internet. See how other people are writing their articles. Notice how short and punchy their sentences are.

4. Get Rid of Fluff
Sometimes, a beginner SEO writer is guilty of padding their article out so they can reach the magical 500-word mark. As such, they start adding fluff to an article which adds no value, but which probably looks good to the writer.

Ergo, they start writing flowery language that demonstrates how eloquent they are. A client will call you out on this straight away. First of all, they don't want you to add fluff just so that you get to 500 words. Secondly, they don't want you to show off your writing skills by using big words. This is not about you and your skills - this is 100% about the reader. If your article has fluff, get rid of it and swap it for something that adds value. An article must contain nothing but value. If there is anything in there that makes you smile, but which is likely to turn a reader (and your client) off, delete it.

5. Be Direct

Another problem that beginner SEO writers wrestle with is clarity. If you can't sum up what an article is all about in the first two sentences, you lose. A client will forgive you this if you're a newbie, but this is something you need to learn quickly. Get straight to the point ASAP. You and the reader are both in a hurry. If you take them sround in circles, they'll soon get impatient and leave the page.

Be direct and obvious about what your intentions are with an article and what you want from them. Don't try to be clever. You'll come across as too vague. The reader won't have a clue what you're trying to tell them, and they'll give up. They certainly won't hang around because you're such a good writer. They don't care that you're a good writer! They only care about what's in it for them.

6. Address the Reader

Another easy mistake you can make as a beginner writer is failing to address and therefore engage your reader.

If the article is about them - which it is - why wouldn't you address them directly? "Hey you! Ever wanted to know the easy way to losing weight?" See?

Better than:

"Many people want to know how to lose weight, but have so far come undone."

Both sentences work, and they can both be used. But the first one is more active and engages your reader better. Let them know you're talking to them. Be friendly, be personable, and tell them you're going to solve their problems.

7. Outline their Problem

Speaking of problems, you must remember at all times that a reader is on your page because they've got a problem that they're hoping you're going to solve for them.

So what do you do? You address the problem as soon as possible (ideally in the opening line, and preferably with a question), before outlining how the article is going to solve it.

Example:

"Looking for an objective review of the 2017 Ford Mustang? We've got you covered, from fired-up engines to finance deals."

We've addressed the customer's problem early on - they're looking for a review of the Ford Mustang - and we've outlined how we're going to solve said problem.

CHAPTER 7: HOW TO AVOID COMMON PROBLEMS

All newbie SEO writers have fallen through trapdoors. The English language is so nuanced that it's easy to get tripped up by it. Even the most seasoned writer can screw up now and again if they're not careful.

Grammar is still sensitive for clients. They only want to pay $5 to newbie SEO writers, but they still get a bit annoyed if your grammar is off. However, there are things they're willing to let slide. Move up to the bigger jobs, though, and a client will be less forgiving. Indeed, they won't give you a job in the first place unless your grammar is on-point.

Is it "it's" or Is it "its"?
Ah, one of the most trifling issues in the English language! When do you use "it's" and when is it appropriate to use "its"?

Basically, "it's" is "it is" joined up. For example: "It's raining today."

"Its" meanwhile is to be used when something belongs to something else. For example: "The little chick always follows its mother."

When Is It "Your" And When Is It "You're"?
People use "your" and "you're" incorrectly all the time. Some non-writers never grow out of this mistake, and will continue making it - especially on Facebook.
If, however, you want to make it as a writer, you need to iron out this mistake right now.

"Your" is possessive. For example: "This is your t-shirt."

"You're," on the other hand, is "you are" joined up. For example: "You're going out tonight?"

It's so simple once you know the difference. Until then, it's such an easy mistake to make.

"To Be" Or Not "Too Be"?
That is the question! And the answer is easy: Too is an adverb that emphasizes something. For example: "That's too much!" or "He was driving too quickly."

Meanwhile, you'll use "to" in pretty much every other situation. For example: "Are we going to the shops?" or "I want to go to the game!"

"There", "Their" Or "They're"

This is a biggie! How many times has this one thrown you?

"They're" is "they are" joined up. For example: "They're coming to dinner tonight."

"Their" is possessive, and usually refers to someone. For example: "I had a great time at their house last night."

"There," meanwhile, is used when you're referring to a location. For example: "My mom is over there."

"Then" Or "Than"
Okay, last one. And this is another one that trips people up.

"Then" is an adverb that references time. For example: "We went out for drinks, and then we went home."

"Than" is usually used when you're comparing things. For example: "It's quicker to ride the bus than it is to walk."

Hopefully you've got a good grasp of all that now. It's important to learn this basic stuff, because otherwise you won't get very far as an SEO writer.

CHAPTER 8: HOW TO PRODUCE FLAWLESS CONTENT

Now that you've gotten a few basic rules of grammar out of the way, you can focus on getting your content up to scratch so that it's so good a client can't help but come back for more work. They might even recommend you to someone else! The better your work is, the more work you will get. And the more work you get, the more you'll get paid.

SEO clients are used to working with average writers. One of the reasons for this is that they don't pay very well. They pay $5 - $10 per 500 words. So what do they expect? But once you start producing top quality work on a regular basis, you really will move up in this world. You'll attract better clients who are prepared to pay you more money.

How do you produce killer content? By taking a look at my tips in this chapter!

1. Know The Facts

The copywriting king David Ogilvy said that the first thing he always did when given a brief was to gather the facts about the topic he was writing about.

Looking at the facts allows you to find an angle in your writing. For example, Ogilvy learned that the loudest feature on a brand new Rolls Royce was its clock. He exploited this, crafting an article that focused on the fact that the car was SO quiet that its clock was its loudest feature! You can imagine how appealing that was to prospective Rolls Royce buyers.

Facts are facts. They are what the reader needs to see before making up their mind about something. Without facts, your article is just opinion. Where's the value in that? Find your facts and then deliver them in an interesting way.

2. Craft A Catchy Headline

Clients will sometimes come up with the headline themselves, but often they won't. And when they don't, it's up to you to craft a catchy headline that grabs a readers attention.

This is one of the most difficult aspects of SEO and copywriting. Your client will probably be satisfied with whatever you come up with, especially if they're not exactly paying top dollar. But if you want to start earning more money, you need to get good at creating the kind of catchy headlines that readers find irresistible.

See, a reader needs a reason to click on your article. They need to know what's in it for them. And they need to know that whatever is in it for them is going to benefit them. Catchy headlines are informative, but they also list benefits. Good ones also contain power words that get people interested. Usually they go something like this:

Sample Headline: 20 Killer Ways To Get Wasps Out Of Your Yard

20 is the number of great tips a reader can expect. Killer is your power word. And getting wasps out of their yard is the problem you're going to solve for them.

3. Outline the Problem in the First Paragraph

A lot of readers don't get beyond the first paragraph. Heck, a lot of readers don't even get beyond the first sentence. To keep your reader on the page for as long as possible, it's super important that you outline their problem in the opening paragraph, along with the solution you've got for them. One technique is to start with a question. For example"

"Getting bugged by all the wasps in your yard? Need a safe way of getting rid of them so they don't come back? I can help. In this article …"

See how that works? You're outlining their problem as soon as possible, as well as letting them know how you're going to solve it.

4. Know your Audience
Who are you writing for? You're not writing for yourself anymore. You're writing for someone else. But who?

When someone first gets into SEO writing, it's not always easy for them to get it into their heads that they're writing for a specific audience. As a consequence, their tone is wrong. This will happen if you don't know who you're writing for.

First, you have to do a character profile on who the article is for. Research your intended audience. What are their interests? How old are they? What do they want? Then, picture them sat in front of you as you write. You don't have to picture yourself typing to an entire auditorium. Just picture one or two people in front of you. It will help you to write content that speaks to them and not someone else.

Getting it out of your head that your articles are not for you is difficult and it will take some time, but it can be done. Just remember that everything you right from now on is for someone else. Adjust your language for them. If they're not going to understand what a big word like "engender" means, then don't use it. If you can't speak a reader's language, you won't get very far.

5. Be Personable and Friendly

The number one rule in SEO writing should be this: Don't Be Boring. Problem is, this is easier said than done when you're new to the game. You're a little nervous, and maybe you don't have much confidence. This can come across in the way you write.

It's important that you write in a friendly, personable tone of voice. Be enthusiastic about your product. Be positive. If you can make a reader feel good about themselves, the product and you, you've got a much better chance of getting them to do what you want them to do. Your client will also appreciate it.

6. Don't Break Momentum

There are copywriters who fail because they don't know how to build momentum. Once they've got a rhythm going and are going places with an article, they decide to take a break. And I don't mean a 5-10 minute break. I mean a 2 - 6 hour break. Some writers even leave things a WHOLE DAY before returning. See, a lot of writers are in the habit of setting themselves a daily goal of 1,000 words. That's fine (although 1,000 words is too little for a day's work).

But if you're starting to build momentum and are bashing out killer content, you must keep going. You're in the zone - why would you leave it? Once you leave the zone, it's really hard to get back into it. Face it, a lot of things have to be in place for you to be inspired. You have to be in a good mood. The day has to start well. There should be no distractions.

What if you wake up tomorrow to pick up where you left off and find that the words just won't come? What if you're saddled by brain fog? It happens. The uniqueness of the job is that your daily disposition changes from one day to the next, and it can affect your writing.

It's good practice to keep writing once you find yourself in the zone. Don't stop, even if you surpass your daily word count. Build momentum. Full steam ahead!

7. Read What Others Are Doing
Another rookie mistake freelance writers make is not studying the work of more experienced writers. If you ignore all the examples of good writing out there, you

won't have any idea what makes a good SEO, copy or content.

You might have a major in English literature. You might have read Dostoevsky, Tolstoy and Melville. But so what? That might sound harsh. But those guys won't help you now. The people who will help you are the pro bloggers and SEO writers.

Read landing pages. Read blogs. Read web content. Read it all voraciously and pick up tips along the way. SEO writers are your heroes now. That might sound really odd, but it's the truth.

8. Paint Pictures
A client has hired you to write for them for one purpose only: they want you to help grow their brand and bag them more conversions.

A great way of improving conversions is by painting pictures in the minds of a reader. See, what you're really trying to do is tap into a reader's emotion. You want them to feel a certain way. It's hard to make someone feel a certain way, but the best method of doing this is by painting pictures in their heads.

Let's say you're selling a convertible car. You might write something like this:

"Picture the scene. You're cruising down the Las Vegas strip. It's 30 degrees Celsius outside. You wind the window down, and the sun kisses your cheeks while a soft wind caresses you. You hang your arm out of the door. Does life get any better?"

It's all about making your readers feel a certain way. If you can make them feel the way you want them to feel, you're winning.

CHAPTER 9: LET'S SET YOUR BUSINESS IN JUST A WEEK

Setting up a business in just a week might seem like a ridiculous notion. But it's only a ridiculous notion if you're an expert at procrastinating.

It's easy to set up a business in just as week. All you need is a plan of action, and some drive. There is an ancient Chinese proverb that sums up most of us:

"The best time to plant a tree was 20 years ago. The second best time is now."

Setting up your own freelance writing business will sound daunting to you right now. But this book is here to help ease your fears and make it easier to get your business off the ground. And it's really important that from now on you start treating what you're doing as a business. Because that's exactly what it is.

Okay, so it's not a business in the same sense that a startup in Silicon Valley is a business. This is a good thing, as it means it won't take as much time to get started. But it's key that you start treating what you're doing as a business from now on.

In this chapter, you'll find a seven-day action plan that will help you to get your business up and running in just a week. This seven-day action plan isn't complicated - it's simple and easy to follow and implement. All I ask is that you have some drive.

Read? Let's go!

Day 1 and 2
Before starting, you need a laptop or a computer, WiFi, and a sound word-processor. Some clients prefer it when you use MS Word, because it's best for formatting. It also means they can edit documents easily. Moreover, some clients find it hard to open RTF files (which is what Text Edit saves files as).

However, most clients aren't fussy about what word processor you use, and you can get away with using Text Edit if it works best for you. Google Docs is an amazing tool that allows you and your client to edit a document at the same time, and indeed more freelancers are using it to write their content. Google Docs also comes in handy if you haven't got MS Word, and can't afford to buy it.

One thing you can't mess around with is WiFi. You need fast Internet speed, and you need a reliable Internet connection. If you're going to cut the costs on something this month, don't make it your Internet service provider. Be prepared to pay the money for a fast, stable connection. If your Internet is slow, it's going to slow you down as you do your research. Not cool. Don't cut the costs here. Spend money on good Internet speed.

The third thing you need to do on your first and second day of setting up your brand new business is set up a payment method. This has proved to be the stumbling block of some young would-be freelance writers. They haven't got a bank account, and thus have no means of getting paid digitally.

You could use PayPal but you'll still need to eventually transfer money from your PayPal account into your bank account. Unless, of course, you buy everything from your PayPal account.

Global freelancing platforms such as Upwork.com don't require you to have a bank account. You can get paid either directly to your bank account, or you can get paid into your PayPal account.

PayPal is fast and secure, and it's a good way of holding onto your money. However, there are transaction fees involved. If a client transfers $100 into your PayPal account, PayPal takes around $6 as a transaction fee. It's not massive, but if every cent counts for you right now, you're better off getting paid directly into your bank account.

On the first day you should also buy a couple of copywriting books off the Internet. Buy them now, and they'll probably arrive by day 7. A few books you can start with include, *Write To Sell* and *Ogilvy On Advertising.*

Days 3 and 4
Never written online content before? Then it's time to write a few sample articles.

All clients ask to see article samples before they hire you. If they don't, they're dodgy. To get an idea of how good you are at writing and whether or not you're the right fit for them, clients will want to see at least one writing sample. So use days three and four to do some writing for a potential client.

Choose subjects you have some knowledge of. If you're into sports, write an article about sports. It could be something like "Top 5 Tennis Players You Need To Watch Out For In 2017."

But don't just stick to one niche. Spread your wings and write about a few different things. This is good because you won't be applying for jobs in one specific niche once you get started for real. As such, you'll need a writing sample for all occasions.

Not sure where to start? Check out some content on the Internet and rewrite it. Rewriting content will help you develop your chops. Find some articles related to a particular niche and put them into your own words. The more you do this, the more you'll develop a taste for the style of writing you're getting involved with. You'll pick up habits related to language, tone and style. It's a great way of learning the ropes.

The easiest articles to start with are listicles. You know the type:

- 10 Ways You Can Save Money On A Budget
- 5 Must-See Movies In 2017
- 7 Texts You Should Never Send A Girl

These are the kind of articles you might be asked to write by clients in the future. Getting some samples smashed out is a good place to start, and will help to strengthen your applications.

As mentioned, it's a good idea to check out content already on the Internet, as it will help you to focus your sample articles. It'll give you insight into how these types of articles begin with their introductions, how they are formatted, the types of subheadings they use, as well as how they end.

Writing samples without looking at previously existing work means you'll largely be fumbling around in the dark.

Day 5

On Day 5, you should start working on your cover letter. The great thing about being a freelance writer is that you don't need a resume.

Now that you're a freelance writer, you don't have to write a resume. All you need is a strong cover letter, and you can spend day 5 working on this.

Your cover letter shouldn't be too long. Use a minimum of two paragraphs and a maximum of four. Keep it nice and tight. Reserve the opening line to talk about the specific job you are applying for. Obviously you can't write about a specific job just yet, because you haven't applied to any. But you could still begin with:

"Hi there! I'm applying for this role because … "

You could then use the second paragraph to talk about yourself and your style of writing. Write about you skills, and what type of writing you usually do (blogs, copy, content, newsletters, eBooks etc). In the third, you could include any past writing experience you have. If you've self-published any books, include this.

Your cover letter is essentially your sales letter, so it has to be well written. It should be engaging, personable, friendly, upbeat, and it should demonstrate in just a few words why you're the writer for them. Let your confidence come out in your cover letter, but avoid clichés. Clients prefer freelancers who are honest, rather than freelancers who have clearly patched up a cover letter with lots of clichés that probably don't reflect who they are.

Day 6
On the sixth day, it's time to finally take the plunge and join a global freelancing platform. This is when things start to get real. There are a few platforms you can use. Most first-time writers go for Freelancer.com, and it's a good place to start.

Setting up your profile could take a few hours, especially if you're an expert procrastinator. But, the sooner you get this nailed, the sooner you can start applying for work and making money.

You won't create the perfect profile straight off the bat, so don't worry too much about that. This is because you learn about what works as you go along. For now, the text in your profile can be similar to your cover letter, but not the same. Add a few different things, and really sell yourself to potential clients. Again, remember to be positive, friendly and approachable.

You will also need a profile picture. Freelancers should always have one. It's annoying because clients often don't have profile pictures, but it figures because we're the ones selling ourselves. Make sure that you looking positive in your profile picture. You don't necessarily have to be smiling, but you definitely don't want to look gloomy. You need to look approachable. You need to look like someone people want to work for.

There will also be tests to take before your profile becomes active. Don't be daunted by these (although some of them are daunting). Just take your time. Once your profile is live you can kick back and relax until Day 7.

Day 7

On the seventh day, it's time for you to start applying for work. Yep, this is it! Good luck! Remember to start with smaller jobs. It might suck, but without much experience you'll find it hard to land the bigger jobs. Moreover, the last thing you need as you start out is the pressure of a $300 job!

CONCLUSION

So there you have it. Becoming a successful freelance writer is totally possible. You can do it. The time is now.

Things might move slowly for a while, and you might be stuck with low-paying jobs for the first few weeks or months. But perseverance is key. The breakthrough will come as long as you stick at it, and keep working on improving your craft.

THANKS FOR READING

We really hope you enjoyed this book. If you found this material helpful feel free to share it with friends. You can also help others find it by leaving a review where you purchased the book. Your feedback will help us continue to write books you love.

The Smart Reads library is growing by the day! Make sure and check out the other wonderful books in our catalog. We would love to hear which books are your favorite.

Visit:
www.smartreads.co/freebooks
to receive Smart Reads books for FREE

Check us out on Instagram:
www.instagram.com/smart_readers
@smart_readers

Don't forget your 2 FREE audiobooks.
Use this link www.audibletrial.com/Travis to claim
your 2 FREE Books.

SMART READS ORIGINS

Smart Reads was born out of the desire to find the best information fast without having to wade through the sheer volume of fluff available online. Smart Reads combs through massive amounts of knowledge compiles the best into quick to read books on a variety of subjects.

We consider ourselves Smart Readers, not dummies. We know reading is smart. We're self taught. We like to learn a TON about a WIDE variety of topics. We have developed a love for books and we find intelligence attractive.

We found that each new topic we tried to learn about started with the challenge of finding the pieces of the puzzle that mattered most. It becomes a treasure hunt rather than an education.

Smart Reads wants to find the best of the best information for you. To condense it into a package that you can consume in an hour or less. So you can read more books about more topics in less time.

OUR MISSION

Smart Reads aims to accelerate the availability of useful information and will publish a high quality book on every major topic on amazon.

Smart Reads hopes to remove barriers to sharing by taking the copyright off everything we publish and donating it to the public domain. We hope other publishers and authors will follow our example.

Our goal is to donate $1,000,000 or more by 2020 to build over 2,000 schools by giving 5% of our net profit to Pencils of Promise.

We want to restore forests around the globe by planting a tree for every 10 physical books we sell and hope to plant over 100,000 trees by 2020.

Doesn't it feel good knowing that by educating yourself you are helping the world be a better place? We think so too...

Thanks for helping us help the world. You Smart Reader you...

Travis and the Smart Reads Team

WHY I STARTED SMART READS

Every time I wanted to learn about something new I'd have to buy 20 books on the topic and spend way too long sorting through them and reading them all until I arrived at the big picture. Until I had enough perspectives to know who was just guessing, who was uninformed and who had stumbled upon something remarkable.

I wished someone else could just go in and figure that out for me and tell me what matters. That's how smart reads was born. I want smart reads to be a company that does all that research up front. Sorts through all the content that is available on each topic and pulls out the most up to date complete understanding, then have people smarter than me package the best wisdom in an easy to understand way in the least amount of words possible.

For example, I got a new puppy so I wanted to learn about dog training. I bought 14 different books about dog training and by the time I got through the first 5 and finally started getting the big picture on the best way to train my puppy she had grown up into a dog.

Yeah she's well behaved. She doesn't poop in the house. I can get her to sit and come when I call. But what if someone else went in and read all those books for me, found the underlying themes and picked out the best information that would give me the big picture and get me right to the point. And I'd only have to read one book instead of 15.

That would be amazing. I would save time. And maybe my dog would be rolling over, cleaning up after my kids and doing the dishes by now. That my friend, is the reason I started smart reads. Because I wanted a company I can trust to deliver me the best information in an easy to understand way that I can digest in under an hour. Because dog training is one of many subjects I want to master.

The quicker I can learn a wide variety of topics the sooner that information can begin playing a role in shaping my future. And none of us knows how long that future will be. So why not do everything we can to make the best of it and consume a ton of knowledge. And I figured all the better if I can also make a positive difference in the world.

That's why we're also building schools, planting trees and challenging ideas about copyright's place in today's world. Because as a company we have to be doing everything we can to support the ecosystem that gives us all these beautiful places to read our books. Thanks for reading.

Travis

Customers Who Bought This Customers Who Bought This Book Also Bought

Passive Income: Do What You Want When You Want and Make Money While You Sleep

Blockchain Revolution: Understanding the Internet of Money

Reinvent Yourself: Become Instantly Likable, Captivate Anyone in Seconds and Always Know What To Say

Mastering Your Time: Learn How Successful People Enhance Productivity, Beat Procrastination and Do More in Less Time

The Everything Store Sales Guide: How to Make Money with Amazon FBA

A Detailed Guide in Building A Successful Photography Business Online: Learn How to Market, Sell, Promote and Make Money as a Photographer

Minimalism: Declutter, Organize and Reclaim your Space